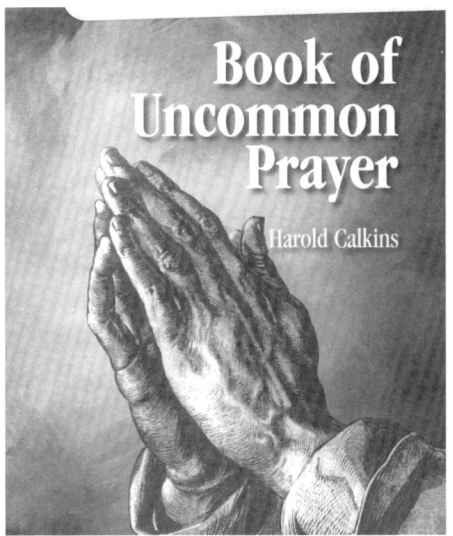

Book of Uncommon Prayer

Harold Calkins

First published 2002
Copyright © 2002
All rights reserved. No part of this publication
may be reproduced in any form without prior
permission from the publisher.

British Library Cataloguing in Publication Data.
A catalogue record for this book is available
from the British Library.

ISBN 1-903921-02-3

Printed and published by
Autumn House Limited
Grantham, Lincs.

Introduction

Prayer engages three sources of energy: Divine, angelic and human. It allows God to work; requires angels to work; and puts us to work.

Prayer quarries gems of character and polishes them into attractive personalities.

Prayer, as Chrysostum says, 'is a mine which is never exhausted, . . . the mother of a thousand blessings.'

Prayer is the breath of the soul. It is to the human spirit what oxygen is to the body. It is the key in the hand of faith to unlock Heaven's storehouse, where are treasured boundless resources of Omnipotence.

Prayer is the most powerful form of energy known to the world.

Archbishop Trench penned words worth memorising that call us, morning, noon and evening, to the experience of prayer:

> Lord, what a change within us one short hour
> Spent in Thy presence would prevail to make!
> What heavy burdens from our bosoms take.
> What parched ground revive as with a shower.
> We kneel, how weak, we rise how full of power.
> Why therefore should we do ourselves this wrong,
> Or others, that we are not always strong!

'Lord, teach us to pray.'

Harold Calkins

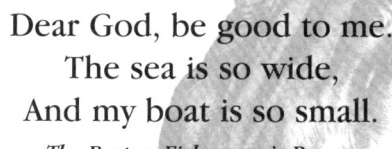

Dear God, be good to me.
The sea is so wide,
And my boat is so small.

The Breton Fishermen's Prayer

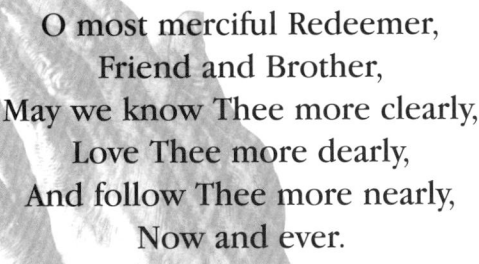

O most merciful Redeemer,
Friend and Brother,
May we know Thee more clearly,
Love Thee more dearly,
And follow Thee more nearly,
Now and ever.

Richard of Chichester

Lord, teach me all that I should know;
In grace and wisdom may I grow;
The more I learn to do Thy will,
The better may I love Thee still.

Isaac Watts, 1674-1748

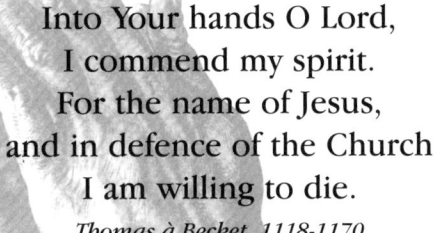

Into Your hands O Lord,
I commend my spirit.
For the name of Jesus,
and in defence of the Church
I am willing to die.

Thomas à Becket, 1118-1170

Good Shepherd, still confessing
Love, in spite of our transgressing –
Here Your blessed food processing,
Make us share Your every blessing
In the land of life and love:
You, whose power has all completed
And Your flesh as food has meted,
Make us at Your table seated
By Your sense, as friends be greeted,
In Your paradise above.

Thomas Aquinas, 1225-1274

Christ be with me, Christ within me,
Christ beneath me, Christ above me,
Christ in quiet, Christ in danger,
Christ in hearts of all that love me,
Christ in mouth of friend or stranger.

Praise to the Lord of my salvation;
Salvation is of Christ the Lord. Amen.

St Patrick, circa 390-circa 461

When You Travel

God be with you in every pass,
Jesus be with you on every hill,
Spirit be with you on every stream,
Headland and ridge and lawn;
Each sea and land,
each moor and meadow,
Each lying down, each rising up,
In the trough of the waves,
on the crest of the billows,
Each step on the journey you go.

Celtic prayer

My Jesus, my King, my life, my all,
I again dedicate my whole self to You.
Accept me, and grant, O gracious Father,
That before this year is over
I may finish my task.
In the name of Jesus I ask it. Amen.

David Livingstone, 1813-1873

Almighty Father, Son and Holy Ghost,
Eternal-blesséd, gracious God,
To me, the least of saints, to me, allow
That I may keep a door in paradise;
That I may keep even the smallest door,
The furthest door, the darkest, coldest door,
If so be it but in Thine house, O God!

Columba, 521-597

Lord God in whom we live and
move and have our being;
Open our eyes so we may see
Your presence always about us.
Draw our hearts to You with the
power of Your love.

B. F. Westcott, 1825-1901

Thine for ever, God of love,
Hear us from Thy throne above.
Thine for ever may we be,
Here and in eternity.

Mary E. Maude, 1819-1913

Lord Jesus Christ,
How often was I impatient,
About to lose heart,
About to give up everything,
About to seek the fearfully easy way out: despair.
But you never lost patience,
You bore a whole life of suffering
To redeem even me.

Søren Kierkegaard, 1813-1855

Thou, Lord, who knowest my heart,
All its desire and all its need,
Show me what Thou art able to do with it,
And do what Thou art able;
Through Jesus Christ.

H. C. G. Moule, 1841-1920

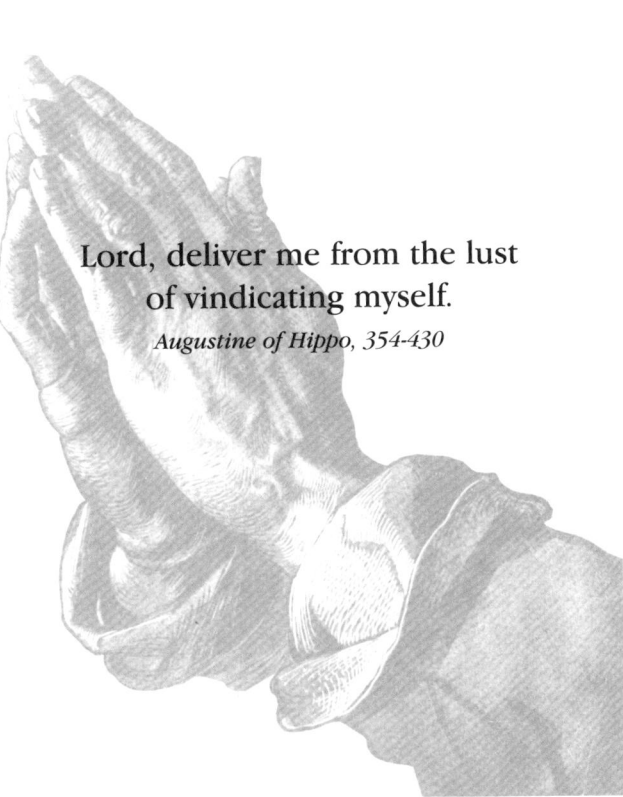

Lord, deliver me from the lust of vindicating myself.
Augustine of Hippo, 354-430

O Lord, grant that I may do
Thy will as if it were my will,
So that Thou mayest do
Thy will as if it were my will.

Augustine of Hippo, 354-430

Lord, make me an
instrument of Thy peace;
Where there is hatred, let me sow love.
Where there is injury, pardon;
Where there is doubt, faith;
Where there is despair, hope;
Where there is darkness, light;
And where there is sadness, joy!

Attributed to St Francis of Assissi, 1182-1226

Divine Master,
grant that I may not so much seek
To be consoled as to console;
To be understood as to understand;
To be loved as to love;
For it is in giving that we receive;
It is in pardoning that we are pardoned;
And it is in dying to self that we are
born to the life everlasting.

Attributed to St Francis of Assissi, 1182-1226

Dear Lord, my Shepherd,
Plentiful Provider,
Thank you for the relaxation of
green pastures.
You quiet my troubled waters,
You revive my soul,
You guide me into the right paths,
Even in death's shadow You comfort me.
My heart overflows with your
goodness and mercy.
I want to live with You, Lord, for ever.

Adapted from Psalm 23

Lord, my God, You have made your servant king instead of David my father, though I am a mere child, unskilled in leadership. . . . Grant your servant an understanding heart so that he may govern Your people justly and distinguish good from evil. Otherwise who is equal to the task of governing this great people of yours?

King Solomon (adapted)

Lord, remember me when
You come into Your kingdom.

Thief on the Cross, Luke 23:42

Lord, may we diligently await
the coming of Your Son.
When He knocks,
may He find us watching in prayer
and rejoicing in His praise who
lives and reigns with You for ever.

George Herbert, 1593-1633

Come my Joy, my Love, my Heart:
   Such a joy, as none can move:
   Such a love, as none can part:
   Such a heart, as joyes in love.

George Herbert, 1593-1633

O Light invisible, we praise Thee!
Too bright for mortal vision.
O greater Light,
we praise Thee for the less;
The eastern light our spires
touch at morning,
The light that slants upon our
western doors at evening,
The twilight over stagnant
pools at batflight,
Moonlight and starlight,
owl and mothlight,
Glow-worm glowlight on a grassblade,
O Light invisible, we worship Thee!

T. S. Eliot, 1888-1965

I take Thee, God the Father
To be my chief end and highest good.
I take Thee, God the Son
To be my Prince and Saviour.
I take Thee, Holy Spirit
To be my Sanctifier, Teacher,
Guide and Comforter.

Philip Henry, for his son Matthew's baptism

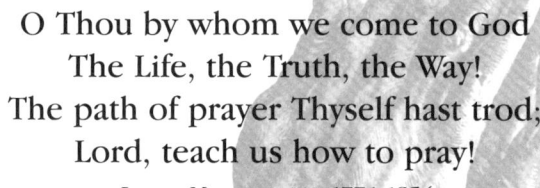

O Thou by whom we come to God
The Life, the Truth, the Way!
The path of prayer Thyself hast trod;
Lord, teach us how to pray!

James Montgomery, 1771-1854

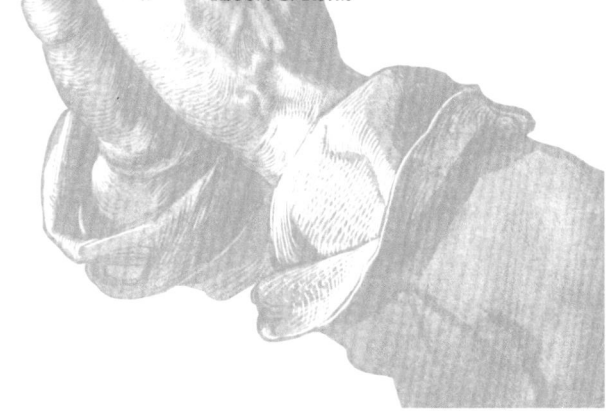

Teach me to pray, Lord, teach me to pray;
This is my heart-cry, day unto day;
I long to know Thy will and Thy way;
Teach me to pray, Lord, teach me to pray.

Albert S. Reitz

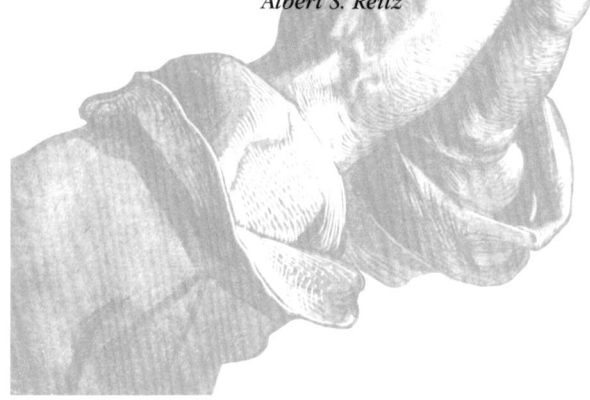

My weakened will, Lord,
Thou canst renew;
My sinful nature, Thou canst subdue;
Fill me just now with power anew;
Power to pray, and power to do.

Albert S. Reitz

O Lord our God, grant us grace to
desire Thee with our whole heart;
That so desiring we may
seek and find Thee;
And so finding Thee may love Thee;
And loving Thee, may hate those sins from
which Thou hast redeemed us.

Anselm, 1033-1109

Master, speak, and make me ready
When Thy voice is truly heard,
With obedience glad and steady
Still to follow every word.

Frances Ridley Havergal, 1836-1879

Heavenly Father, we bow in Your presence;
May Your word be our rule,
Your Spirit our Teacher,
And Your greater glory
our supreme concern;
Through Jesus Christ our Lord.

John Stott, born 1921

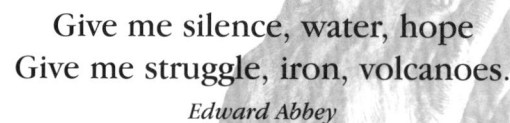

Give me silence, water, hope
Give me struggle, iron, volcanoes.
Edward Abbey

Let not Thy word, O Lord,
become a judgement upon us,
that we hear it and do it not,
that we know it and love it not,
that we believe it and obey it not.

Attributed to Thomas à Kempis, 1380-1471

God grant me the serenity to accept
the things I cannot change,
the courage to change the things I can,
and the wisdom to know the difference.

Reinhold Neihbur (1892-1971)

Lord, it is our chief complaint
that our love is weak and faint;
Yet we love You and adore;
O for grace to love You more.

William Cowper, 1731-1800

Return, O heavenly dove, return
Sweet Messenger of Rest;
We hate the sins that made you mourn,
And drove you from our breast.

William Cowper, 1731-1800

O Thou God that heard
Solomon in the night
when he prayed for wisdom, hear me;
I cannot lead this people:
I cannot guide the affairs of this
nation without Thy help.
I am poor and weak and sinful.

Abraham Lincoln, 1808-1865

Dear Lord, Teach me to be generous;
To give and not to count the cost,
To work and not to seek for any reward,
Save that of knowing that I do Your will.

Ignatius Loyola, 1495-1556

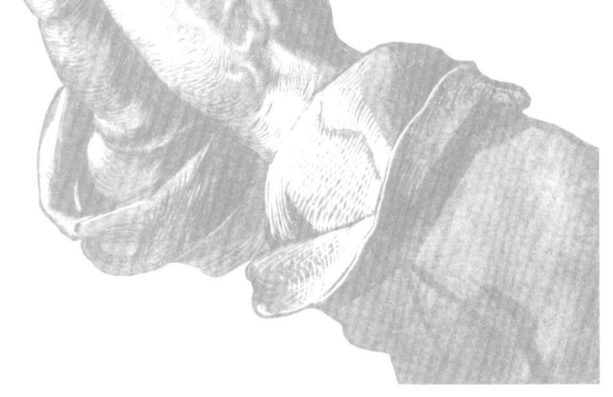

Bless all the children, far and near,
Please keep them safe and free from fear.
So help me sleep and help me wake,
In peace and health, for Jesus' sake.

Children's Prayer

Lord of the loving heart,
May mine be loving too.
Lord of the gentle hands,
May mine be gentle too.
Lord of the willing feet,
May mine be willing too.
So may I grow more like Thee
In all I say and do.

Unknown

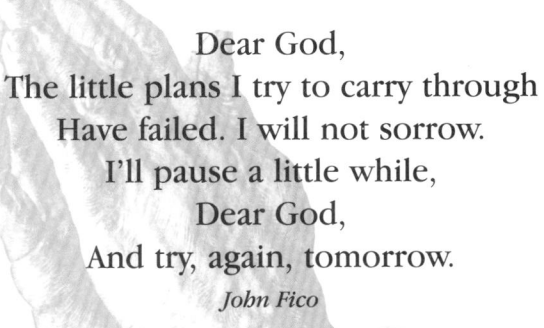

Dear God,
The little plans I try to carry through
Have failed. I will not sorrow.
I'll pause a little while,
Dear God,
And try, again, tomorrow.

John Fico

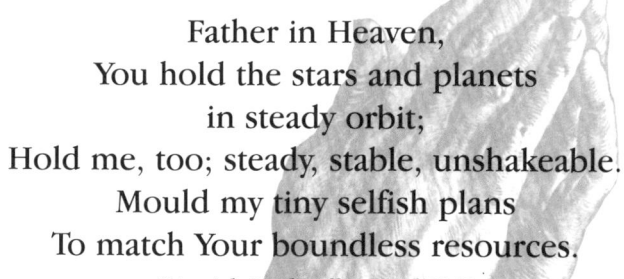

Father in Heaven,
You hold the stars and planets
in steady orbit;
Hold me, too; steady, stable, unshakeable.
Mould my tiny selfish plans
To match Your boundless resources.

Dietrich Bonhoeffer, 1906-1945

Lord Jesus Christ,
You were poor and in distress,
a captive and forsaken as I am.
You know all men's troubles;
You abide with me
when all others have deserted me.

Dietrich Bonhoeffer, 1906-1945

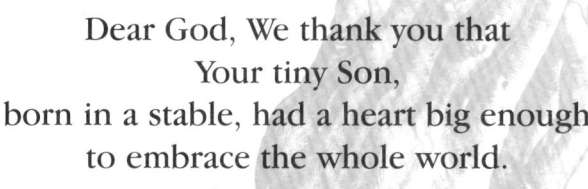

Dear God, We thank you that
Your tiny Son,
born in a stable, had a heart big enough
to embrace the whole world.

Dietrich Bonhoeffer, 1906-1945

Lord, teach me all that I should know;
In grace and wisdom I may grow;
The more I learn to do Thy will,
The better may I love Thee still.

Isaac Watts, 1674-1748

Oh use me, Lord, use even me,
Just as Thou wilt, and when, and where:
Until Thy blessed face I see,
Thy rest, Thy joy, Thy glory share.

Frances Ridley Havergal, 1836-1879

Lamb of God, I look to Thee;
Thou shalt my Example be;
Thou art gentle, meek and mild,
Thou wast once a little child.

Charles Wesley, 1707-1788

Lord, to Thee I kneel and pray,
Pardon all my sins this day.
When I sleep and when I wake
Bless me for my Saviour's sake.

Unknown

Lord, keep us safe this night
Secure from all our fears;
May angels guard us while we sleep
Till morning light appears.

John Leland (1754-1841)

Martyrs' Prayer

Good Lord, give me the grace,
in all my fear and agony,
To have recourse to that great fear
and wonderful agony that You, my Saviour,
Had on the Mount of Olives
before Your most bitter passion;
And in meditating thereon,
to receive spiritual comfort
and consolation profitable for my soul.

Sir Thomas More, 1478-1535

Restore me to liberty,
and enable me so to live now
That I may answer before
You and before me.
Lord, whatever this day may bring,
Your name is to be praised.

Dietrich Bonhoeffer, 1906-1945

Lord, we beseech You to
help and defend us.
Deliver the oppressed, pity the poor,
Uplift those who have fallen,
be the portion of those in need,
return to Your care those
who have gone astray,
feed the hungry, and strengthen the weak.
May all the people come to
know that You alone are God.

Clement of Rome, died circa AD100

O Lord, remember not only the
men and women of good will,
But also those of ill will.
But, do not remember all of the suffering
They have inflicted upon us:
Instead remember the fruits we have borne
Because of this suffering.

*Unknown. Found in the clothing of a
dead child at Ravensbrük*

Grant me to impart willingly to others
whatever I possess that is good and to ask
humbly of others that I may
partake of the good of
which I am destitute.

Thomas Aquinas, 1225-1274

Eternal God, eternal Trinity, You are a mystery as deep as the sea; the more I search, the more I find, and the more I find, the more I search for You.

Catherine of Siena, 1347-1380

Give me the grace, good Lord:
To set the world at naught,
to set the mind firmly on You and not
to hang upon the words of men's mouths;
to be content to be solitary;
not to long for worldly pleasures;
little by little, utterly to cast off the world
and rid my mind of all its business;
for the winning of Christ.

Sir Thomas More, 1478-1535
Prayer in the Tower of London

O Lord, take not Thy Holy Spirit from me;
take away the heart of stone, and give
me a heart of flesh; that under Thy
chastisements I may lift up to
Thee a humble, reverential,
and even a thankful eye.

William Wilberforce, 1759-1833

Lord, though I am a miserable and wretched creature, I come to Thee for grace, and I come to Thee for Thy people. Thou hast made me, though very unworthy, a mean instrument to do them some good, and Thee service. Lord, however Thou do dispose of me, continue to do good for them.

Oliver Cromwell, 1599-1658, on his deathbed

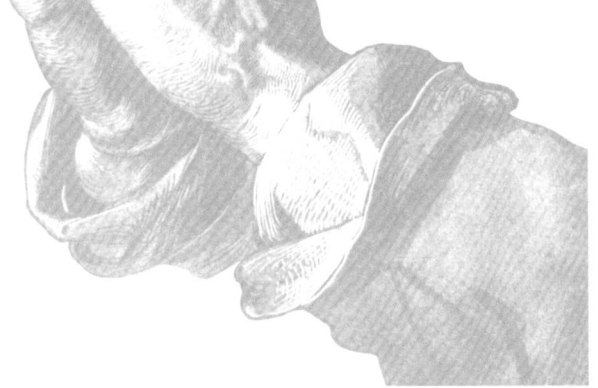

O God, send us the Holy Ghost,
   Give us a bath of spiritual life
   And a fire of unconquerable zeal
Till nations shall yield to the sway of Jesus.

Charles Haddon Spurgeon, 1834-1892

Today, Lord, I hear You say
that with Your help
I can achieve Your ideals for me.
Thank you for giving me that help.
Thank you that all Your
biddings are enablings
That higher than my thoughts can reach
are Your ideals for me

H. C.

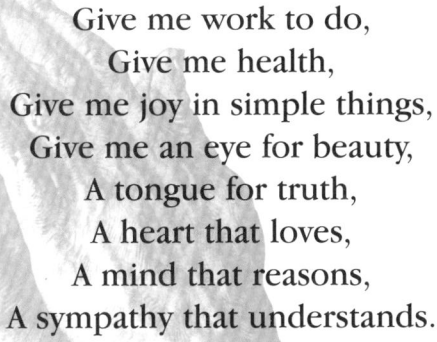

Give me work to do,
Give me health,
Give me joy in simple things,
Give me an eye for beauty,
A tongue for truth,
A heart that loves,
A mind that reasons,
A sympathy that understands.

Unknown

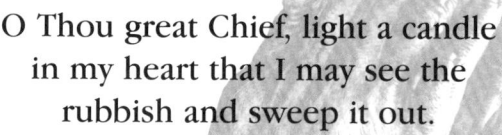

O Thou great Chief, light a candle in my heart that I may see the rubbish and sweep it out.

A Zulu girl who gave her heart to Christ

Thy way, not mine, O Lord!
However dark it be;
Lead me by Thine own hand,
Choose out the path for me.

Smooth let it be, or rough,
It will be still the best;
Winding or straight it matters not,
It leads me to Thy rest.

Horatius Bonar, 1808-1889

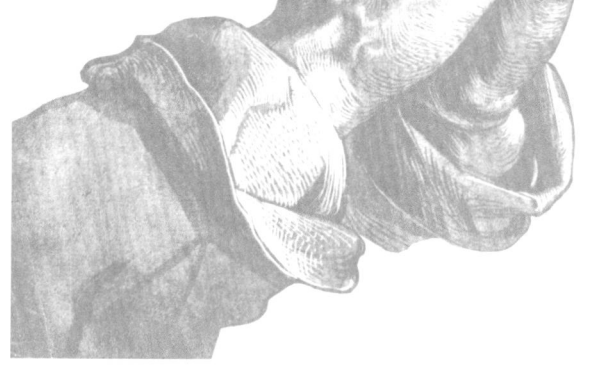

God in Heaven,
Let me really feel my nothingness,
Not in order to despair over it,
But in order to feel the more powerfully
The greatness of Your goodness.

Søren Kierkegaard, 1813-1855

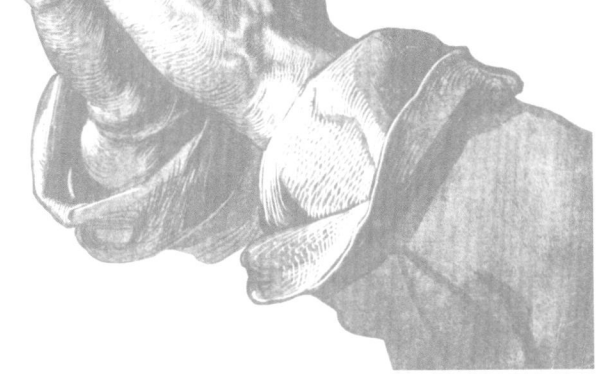

O Saviour! Teach me to turn from my own
fickle and changeful heart, and count more
absolutely and constantly on God.
May I learn not only to pray to Him;
teach me to reckon on His faithfulness.

F. B. Meyer, 1847-1929

Evening Prayer

Hear my prayer, O Heavenly Father,
E'er I lay me down to sleep;
Bid Thine angels, pure and holy,
Round my bed their vigil keep.
Keep me through this night of peril
Underneath its boundless shade;
Take me to Thy rest, I pray Thee,
When my pilgrimage is made.

Charles Dickens, 1812-1870

Prayer for Healing

My Lord and my God,
I have a thousand arguments
against healing prayer.
You are the one argument for it.
You win.
Help me to be a conduit through which
Your healing love can flow to others.

Unknown

Keep me, O Lord, from waxing mentally
and spiritually dull. Help me to keep
the physical, mental and spiritual fibre
of the athlete, of the man who denies
himself daily and takes up his cross.
Give me success in my work,
but hide pride from me.
Save me from the complacency
that so frequently accompanies
success and prosperity.

Samuel Logan Brengle

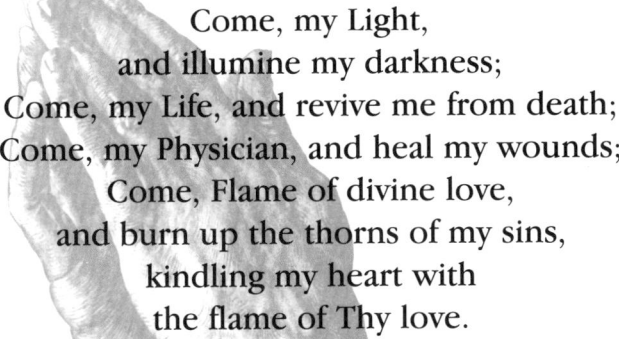

Come, my Light,
and illumine my darkness;
Come, my Life, and revive me from death;
Come, my Physician, and heal my wounds;
Come, Flame of divine love,
and burn up the thorns of my sins,
kindling my heart with
the flame of Thy love.

St Dimitri

Slay utterly, O Lord, and cast down the sin which does so easily beset us; bridle the unholy affection; stay the unlawful thoughts; chasten the temper; regulate the spirit; and, above all, correct the tongue!

Richard S. Brooke, 1835-1893

Make me to remember, O God, that every day is Thy gift and ought to be used according to Thy command. Grant me, therefore, so to repent of my negligence that I may obtain mercy from thee, and pass the time which Thou shalt yet allow me in diligent performance of Thy commands.

Samuel Johnson, 1709-1784

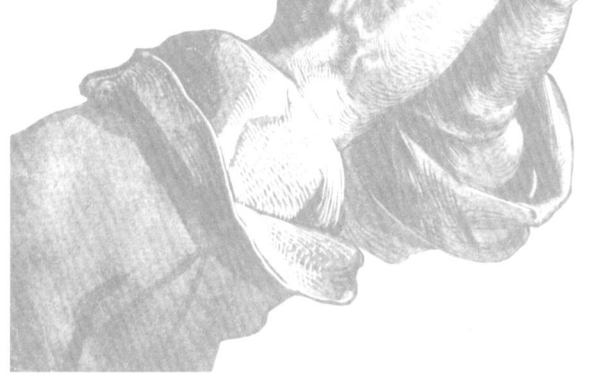

Jesus, keep Thy child today, take me under Thy guardianship, make me a healthy, fruit-bearing branch of the Living Vine.

Ellen G. White, 1827-1915

> We are lost in the fog: have pity on us and teach us the right path.... Make anew those whose bodies are rotten, that they may become sons of God.
>
> *Toyohiko Kagawa, 1888-1960*

Open our hearts, O Lord, and enlighten us
by Thy grace, that we may seek what is
well pleasing to Thy will;
and so order our doings after
Thy commandments,
that we may be found meet
to enter into Thine unending joys.

The Venerable Bede, circa 673-735

From all my lame defeats and oh! much more
From all the victories that I seemed to score;
From the cleverness shot forth on Thy behalf
At which, while angels weep, the audience laugh;
From all my proofs of Thy divinity;
Thou, who wouldst give no sign, deliver me.

C. S. Lewis, 1898-1963

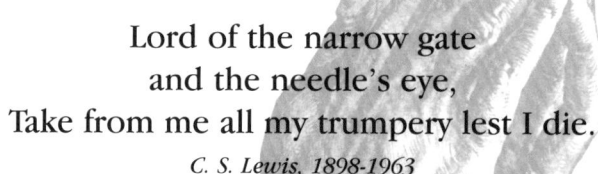

Lord of the narrow gate
and the needle's eye,
Take from me all my trumpery lest I die.

C. S. Lewis, 1898-1963

Lord Jesus,
Risen from the dead and
alive for evermore;
Stand in our midst today
as in the upper room;
Show us Your hands and Your side;
Speak Your peace to our hearts and minds;
And send us forth into the world as
Your witnesses;
For the glory of Your name.

John Stott, born 1921

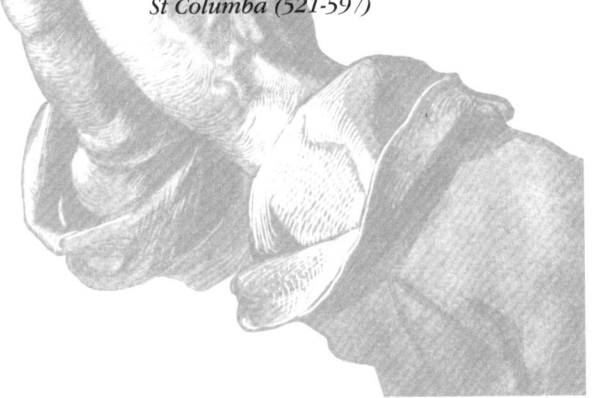

My dearest Lord,
be Thou a bright flame before me,
be Thou a guiding star above me,
be Thou a smooth path beneath me,
be Thou a kindly shepherd behind me,
today and for evermore.

St Columba (521-597)

Lord Jesus,
Risen, ascended and glorified Lord,
We worship You. And as You stand in our
midst through Your Spirit today,
We pray that You will open
our eyes to see You,
Our ears to hear Your voice,
Our hearts to receive Your grace,
And our lips to sing Your praise,
For the glory of Your great name.

John Stott, born 1921

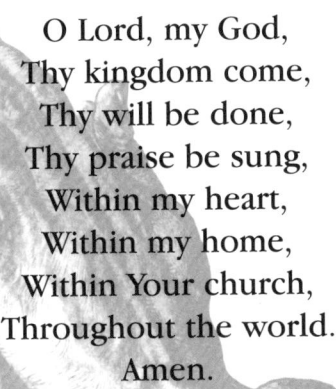

O Lord, my God,
Thy kingdom come,
Thy will be done,
Thy praise be sung,
Within my heart,
Within my home,
Within Your church,
Throughout the world.
Amen.

David Marshall, born 1946

Stand by me, O God, in the name of Thy Son, Jesus Christ, who shall be my Defence and Shelter, yea, my Mighty Fortress, through the might and strength of Thy Holy Spirit. God help me. Amen.

Martin Luther, 1483-1546

Spare not the stroke!
Do with us as Thou wilt!
Let there be naught unfinished,
broken, marred;
Complete Thy purpose,
that we may become
Thy perfect image, O our God and Lord.

Horatius Bonar, 1808-1889

Teach me to dance to the sounds of
Your world and Your people,
I want to move in rhythm with Your plan,
Help me to try to follow Your leading
To risk even falling,
To rise and keep trying,
Because You are leading the dance.

Unknown

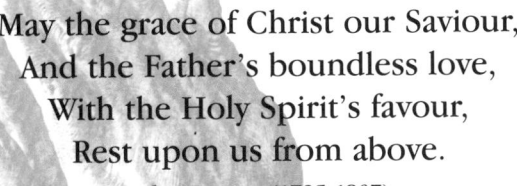

May the grace of Christ our Saviour,
And the Father's boundless love,
With the Holy Spirit's favour,
Rest upon us from above.

John Newton (1725-1807)

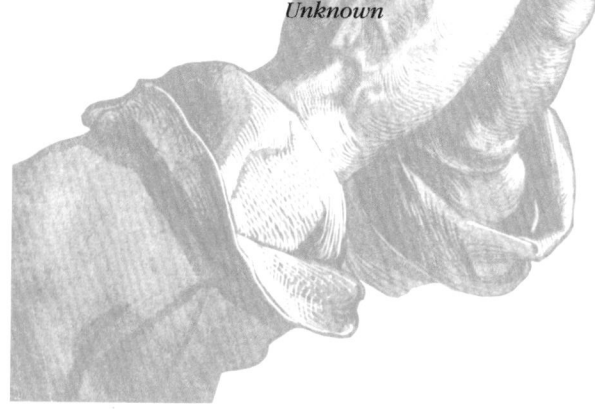

Dear Father,
Hear and bless Thy beasts
and singing birds;
And guard with tenderness small things
That have no words.

Unknown

Dear God, count me in.
Your friend, Herbie.

Linkletter, *Kids Say the Darndest Things*
(Published G. K. Hall)

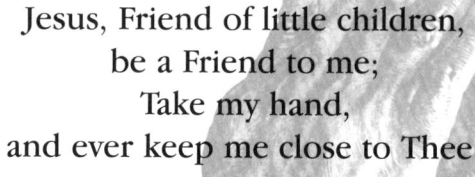

Jesus, Friend of little children,
be a Friend to me;
Take my hand,
and ever keep me close to Thee.
Walter Mathams

Thank You for the world so sweet;
Thank You for the food we eat;
Thank You for the birds that sing;
Thank You, God, for everything!

E. Tutter Leatham

Forgive us our trashbaskets, as we forgive those who put trash in our baskets!

Linkletter, *Kids Say the Darndest Things* (G. K. Hall)

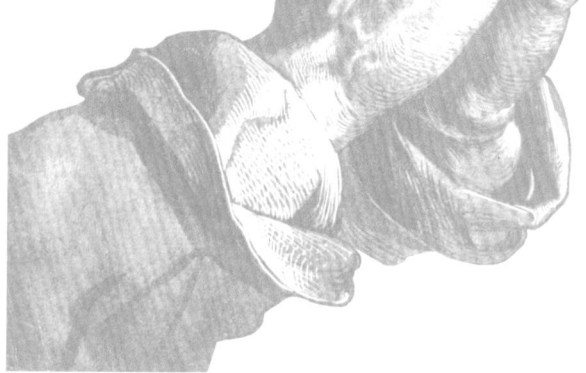

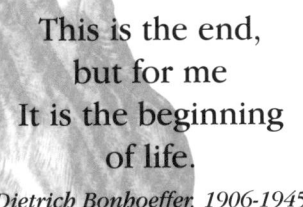

This is the end,
but for me
It is the beginning
of life.

Dietrich Bonhoeffer, 1906-1945

Keep me, O God, from pettiness.
Let me be large in thought, word and
deed. Amen.

Basil, Bishop of Caesarea, 320-379

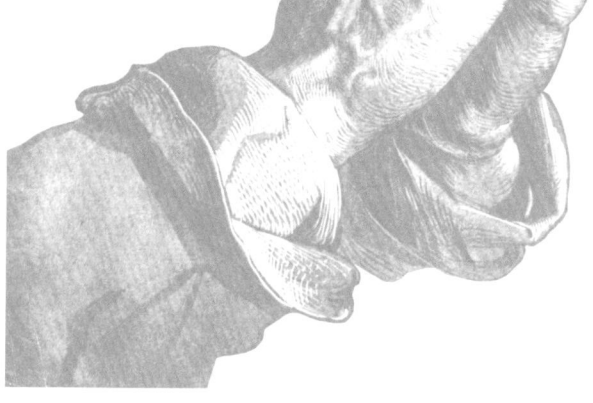

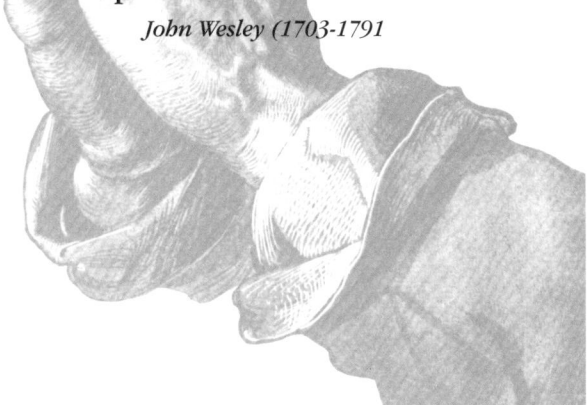

Be gracious to all that are near and dear to me and keep us all in Thy fear and love. Guide us, good Lord, and govern us by the same Spirit, that we may be so united to Thee here as not to be divided when You are pleased to call us hence.

John Wesley (1703-1791

Show me, O Lord, Your mercy.
Behold, I am the man the robbers seized
and left for dead on the road to Jericho.
O kind-hearted Samaritan, come to my aid.

Jerome, 343-420

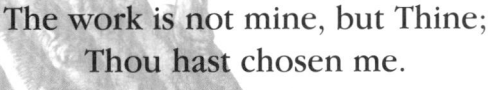

The work is not mine, but Thine;
Thou hast chosen me.
I know it.
Therefore accomplish Thine own will.
Amen.

Martin Luther, 1483-1546

O Lord God, I beseech Thee for Thy mercy's sake to pardon all my enemies. Thou knowest I have been unjustly accused and condemned, but do Thou forgive them this sin.

Jan Huss, 1373-1415, just before he was burned for his faith

Lord, paint on the screen of my mind
the qualities You want me
to actualise today.
You are the Master Artist;
You can paint my life beautiful.
I submit to the touch of Your brush.

H. C.

I praise You for a mind to respond
lovingly to Yours.
May the words I speak and the
thoughts I think
be pleasing to You and
encouraging to others.

H. C.

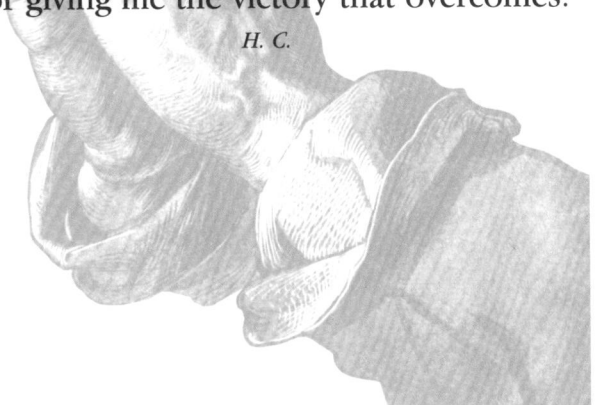

Thank you, Lord,
for picking me up when I stumble,
For healing my hurts when I'm bruised;
For renewing my faith when I fail;
For reviving my spirit when I'm weary;
For giving me the victory that overcomes.

H. C.

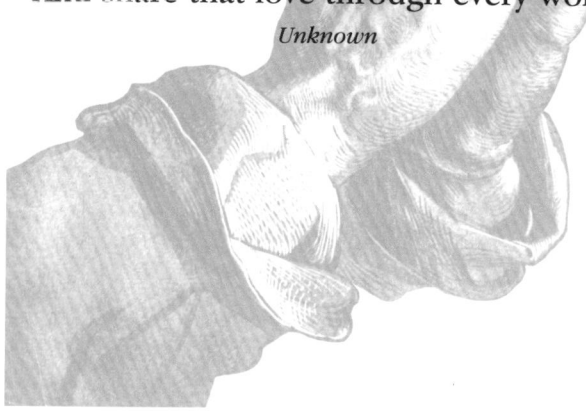

Lord of life, of man and wife,
Father of boys and girls,
Bless this home that moulds their life,
Bless freckled face and auburn curls,
Help them grow to love their Lord,
And share that love through every word.

Unknown

O Master! Deign this church to bless,
This house of prayer, this home of rest.
And let its doors a gateway be,
To lead us from ourselves to Thee.

John Greenleaf Whittier, 1807-1892

Our Father, God of Abraham, of Moses,
Of Daniel, David, Elijah,
And Father of our Lord Jesus Christ,
Thy call hast reached me;
I respond to Thy saving love;
I surrender to Thy claim
– to my time
– to my money
– to my loving devotion. Amen.

H. C.

May we esteem Thee fairer
than all on Earth,
And of more value than great riches.
We pray in the spirit of the
One who became poor,
that we might be eternally rich.

H. M. S. Richards (1894-1985)

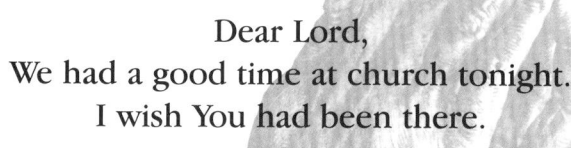

Dear Lord,
We had a good time at church tonight.
I wish You had been there.
4-year-old at his bedtime prayers

Dear God, Our country needs Thee
To help and heal and bless,
To give the rulers wisdom,
To grant the right success,
To feed her many millions,
To keep her always free,
To lead them in the way of Christ,
Where they may walk with Thee.

Unknown

Grant me, O Lord, to face the rain
And not too bitterly complain;
Nor let a joy
My calm destroy;
But teach me so to live that I
Can brother with each passerby.

Edgar A. Guest

Only, O Lord, in Thy dear love
Fit us for perfect rest above;
And help us this and every day,
To live more nearly as we pray.

John Keble, 1792-1866

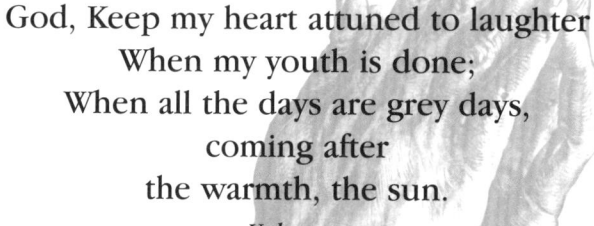

God, Keep my heart attuned to laughter
When my youth is done;
When all the days are grey days,
coming after
the warmth, the sun.

Unknown

A Preacher's Prayer

Help us preachers, Lord, to know
We must mirror, we must show,
Unto all the world Your face;
Unto humankind Your grace.

There's no message we can bring,
There's no song that we can sing,
That shall bring such peace unto
The world as just reflecting You!

William L. Stidger

And now unto Him who is able to keep us from falling and lift us from the valley of despair to the mountains of hope, from the midnight of desperation to the daybreak of joy; to Him be power and authority, for ever.

Martin Luther King, 1929-1968

Lord Jesus, Thou hast said, 'Take my yoke'.
I believe that Thou art willing to tread
Beside me, the hard soil of this Earth!
May I share Thy ploughing
and sowing here,
That I may participate, hereafter,
in Thy golden harvest.

F. B. Meyer, 1847-1929

Most gracious God,
teach me to do Thy will,
Make Thy way clear
and plain before my face,
Help me to run with
patience along the path
That Thou hast marked out for me.

F. B. Meyer, 1847-1929

Lord!
No problem is too big
For Your power.
No person is too small
For Your love!
Hallelujah!
Unknown

Watch, Lord,
With those who wake,
Or watch, or weep tonight,
And give Your angels charge over
Those who sleep.
Tend to Your sick ones, O Lord,
Rest Your weary ones;
Bless Your dying ones;
Soothe Your suffering ones;
Pity Your afflicted ones;
Shield Your joyous ones.
And all for Your love's sake.

Augustine of Hippo, 354-430

Bible Prayers

Lord, I believe, help my unbelief!
Mark 9:24, Revised Authorised Version

God be merciful to me a sinner.
Luke 18:13, RAV

Give me this living water
to satisfy my thirst.
John 4:15, adapted

You are worthy,
O Lord, to receive glory and
honour and power; for You
created all things.
Revelation 4:11, RAV

Lord, take our minds
and think through them;
take our lips and speak through them;
take our hearts and set them on fire
with the desire to do Your holy will.

A student's prayer

Open my eyes that I may see,
Incline my heart that I may desire,
Order my steps that I may follow
The way of Your commandments.

Lancelot Andrewes (1555-1626)

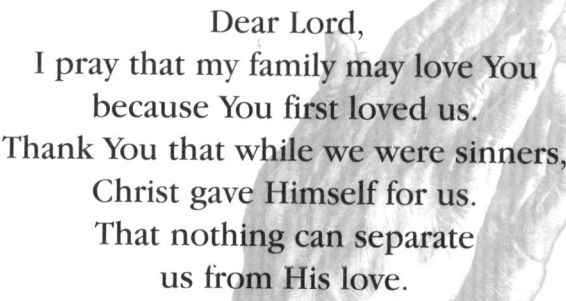

Dear Lord,
I pray that my family may love You
because You first loved us.
Thank You that while we were sinners,
Christ gave Himself for us.
That nothing can separate
us from His love.

Based on 1 John 4:19; Romans 5:8; 8:38, 39

Lord Jesus, in whom the family of Earth
And the family of Heaven are made one;
May every member of my family be
born again into Your family.
May our family live, not by bread alone,
But by every word You have
given us in the Bible.
We pray that Your word be
profitable to instruct us
In right living, reprove us, correct us,
And equip us for all good work.

Based on 1 Peter 1:23; Matthew 4:4; 2 Timothy 3:16

I pray that You will instruct my children
And teach them the way to go,
That You will guide them with
Your eye upon them.
In time of danger or of elation
Help them to hear Your word, saying,
'This is the way, walk in it.'

Based on Isaiah 30:21; Psalm 32:8

Lord, help me to look to Jesus,
The Author and Finisher of my faith.
Help me fight the good fight of faith,
And keep the faith and receive the crown
Which You, the righteous Judge, will give
To all who love Your appearing.

Based on Hebrews 12:2; 2 Timothy 4:7, 8

Lord, Bless all means that are used for my recovery, and restore me to my health in Thy good time; but if otherwise Thou hast appointed for me,
Thy blessed will be done.

Thomas Ken, 1637-1711

Dear Jesus, Come into my life
And let Your beauty be seen in me;
Make my life beautiful as You see beauty;
May Your love brighten my eyes
And quicken my step
And straighten my spine
And paint a smile on my lips
And a song in my heart
For Your glory.

H.C.

The Morning

For this new morning and its light,
For rest and shelter of the night,
For health and food, for love and friends,
For every gift Your goodness sends,
We thank You, gracious Lord.

Unknown

For Food

Be present at our table, Lord,
Be here and everywhere adored:
Thy creatures bless, and grant that we
May feast in paradise with Thee.

John Cennick (1718-1755)

Glory to Thee, my God, this night
For all the blessings of the light;
Keep me, O keep me, King of kings,
Beneath Thine own almighty wings.
Forgive me, Lord, for Thy dear Son,
The ill that I this day have done,
That with the world, myself and Thee
I, e'er I sleep, at peace may be.

Thomas Ken (1637-1711)